MODERN PHP AND

DATABASE-DRIVEN WEB DEVELOPMENT SECRETS

OLIVER LUCAS JR

TABLE OF CONTENTS

Chapter 10

Preface

Welcome to **Modern PHP and MySQL: Database-Driven Web Development Secrets**! This book is your guide to unlocking the power of PHP and MySQL to build dynamic, interactive, and secure web applications. Whether you're a beginner taking your first steps into web development or an experienced programmer seeking to deepen your skills, this book provides a comprehensive and practical journey into the world of server-side programming.

In today's digital landscape, web applications are the driving force behind countless businesses, services, and online experiences. PHP, a versatile and widely-used server-side scripting language, combined with the robustness of MySQL, a leading relational database management system, provides a powerful foundation for building modern web applications.

This book takes a practical, hands-on approach, guiding you through the essential concepts, techniques, and best practices for developing database-driven web applications. We'll start with the fundamentals of PHP and MySQL, covering core syntax, database design, and secure coding practices. Then, we'll delve into building dynamic web applications, exploring topics like user authentication, API development, and performance optimization.

What sets this book apart?

Modern Approach: We focus on modern PHP features and best practices, ensuring you learn the most relevant and efficient techniques.

Security Focus: Security is woven throughout the book, emphasizing secure coding practices to protect your applications from common vulnerabilities.

Practical Examples: Numerous code examples and real-world scenarios illustrate key concepts and provide hands-on experience.

Comprehensive Coverage: We cover a wide range of topics, from basic syntax to advanced techniques, providing a complete guide to PHP and MySQL web development.

Who is this book for?

Aspiring Web Developers: If you're new to web development, this book provides a solid foundation in PHP and MySQL.

Students: This book serves as a valuable resource for students learning web development and database management.

Experienced Programmers: Even seasoned developers will find valuable insights and techniques to enhance their PHP and MySQL skills.

What will you learn?

Master the fundamentals of PHP and MySQL.

Design efficient database schemas.

Build secure user authentication systems.

Develop RESTful APIs for data exchange.

Create dynamic and interactive user interfaces.

Optimize application performance and security.

Deploy your applications to web servers.

Implement version control with Git.

Embrace continuous integration and deployment (CI/CD).

As you embark on this journey, remember that web development is a constantly evolving field. Embrace the challenge of continuous learning, explore new technologies, and stay curious. This book equips you with the foundational knowledge and practical skills to thrive in the exciting world of web development.

Let's begin!

Chapter 1

Modern PHP Essentials

1.1 The Evolution of PHP: From Scripting Language to Powerful Engine

Imagine the early days of the web. Static pages, limited interactivity, a digital landscape yearning for dynamism.[1] Enter Rasmus Lerdorf, a Danish-Greenlandic programmer with a need to track visitors to his online resume.[2] In 1994, he crafted a set of simple tools using the Perl language, christening them "Personal Home Page Tools" - the seed that would blossom into PHP.[3]

This early incarnation, PHP/FI (Forms Interpreter), was far from the sophisticated language we know today.[4] It was a collection of Perl scripts, capable of basic tasks like processing form data and embedding SQL queries. Yet, it held a spark of innovation, a hint of the transformative power to come.

Lerdorf, recognizing the potential of his creation, generously released PHP/FI as open-source. This decision proved pivotal, inviting a community of developers to contribute, experiment, and propel PHP's evolution.[5]

In 1998, PHP underwent a metamorphosis with the release of PHP 3. Andi Gutmans and Zeev Suraski, two Israeli developers, rebuilt the parser from the ground up, laying the foundation for a truly robust scripting language.[6] PHP 3 boasted improved performance, support for a wider range of databases, and a more modular architecture. It was a coming-of-age moment, marking PHP's ascent as a serious contender in the realm of web development.

The momentum continued with PHP 4 in 2000.[7] This version introduced the Zend Engine, a powerful execution engine developed by Gutmans and Suraski.[8] The Zend Engine significantly boosted performance and stability, paving the way for more complex and demanding web applications.[9] PHP 4 also embraced object-oriented programming (OOP) principles, allowing developers to write more structured and reusable code.[10]

PHP 5, released in 2004, was a giant leap forward.[11] With the Zend Engine 2 at its core, it delivered even greater performance gains and introduced a host of new features.[12] Enhanced OOP capabilities, exception handling, and XML support made PHP 5 a versatile and powerful tool for web developers.[13] This era also witnessed the rise of influential PHP frameworks like Symfony and Zend Framework, further solidifying PHP's position in the web development landscape.[14]

The relentless pursuit of performance culminated in PHP 7 (2015). Powered by the Zend Engine 3, PHP 7 delivered a dramatic performance boost, often surpassing even compiled languages like C++ in certain benchmarks.[15] This release prioritized speed, efficiency, and reduced memory consumption, making PHP a compelling choice for high-traffic websites and resource-intensive applications.

Today, PHP continues to evolve. PHP 8, with its just-in-time (JIT) compiler and modern features like attributes and union types, pushes the boundaries of performance and developer productivity.[16] The language remains a cornerstone of the web, powering millions of websites, from small blogs to enterprise-level applications.[17]

The journey of PHP is a testament to the power of open-source collaboration and continuous innovation. From its humble origins as a set of personal tools to its current status as a robust and versatile language, PHP has played a pivotal role in shaping the web as we know it.[18]

1.2 Setting Up Your Development Environment: Tools and Best Practices

Embarking on your PHP and MySQL journey requires a well-equipped and organized workspace. Think of your development environment as your digital workshop, where you'll craft dynamic web applications. This chapter guides you through setting up this space for optimal efficiency and productivity.

1. Choosing Your Operating System

While PHP and MySQL can run on various operating systems (Windows, macOS, Linux), a Linux-based environment often provides the closest match to a live web server. Consider using a Linux distribution like Ubuntu or Debian, or utilize a virtual machine to simulate a Linux environment on your existing system.

2. Installing a Web Server

PHP requires a web server to interpret and execute your code. Apache and Nginx are popular choices, renowned for their reliability and performance. You can install them directly on your system or opt for a pre-configured solution like XAMPP or WAMP, which bundle Apache, MySQL, and PHP for easy setup.

3. Setting Up PHP

Download the latest stable version of PHP from the official website (php.net). Follow the installation instructions for your chosen operating system and web server. Ensure that PHP is correctly configured and integrated with your web server.

4. Installing MySQL

MySQL, our database of choice, can be downloaded from the official MySQL website (mysql.com). During installation, choose a secure root password and remember it—you'll need it to access your database server.

5. Selecting a Code Editor

A good code editor is your digital workbench. Popular choices for PHP development include:

VS Code: A free, open-source editor with excellent PHP support and a vast library of extensions.

Sublime Text: A fast and lightweight editor with a customizable interface.

PHPStorm: A powerful IDE specifically designed for PHP development, offering advanced features like code completion, debugging, and refactoring.

6. Command Line Proficiency

The command line interface (CLI) is a powerful tool for managing your development environment. Familiarize yourself with basic commands for navigating directories, creating files, and executing scripts.

7. Version Control with Git

Git is an essential tool for tracking changes to your code and collaborating with others. Install Git and learn the basics of creating repositories, committing changes, and branching.

8. Local Development Domains

Using a tool like XAMPP, you can set up virtual hosts to access your projects via custom domain names (e.g., myproject.local) instead of relying on generic localhost URLs.

9. Organized File Structure

Maintain a clean and organized file structure for your projects. Separate folders for PHP code, HTML templates, CSS stylesheets, and JavaScript files will make your projects easier to manage and maintain.

10. Regular Backups

Safeguard your work by regularly backing up your projects. Use cloud storage services or external drives to ensure your code is protected in case of hardware failure or accidental deletion.

By following these best practices, you'll create a robust and efficient development environment, setting the stage for your successful journey into the world of PHP and MySQL web development.

1.3 Core Syntax and Constructs: Variables, Operators, and Control Flow

Now that you've set up your development environment, it's time to delve into the building blocks of PHP – the essential syntax and constructs that empower you to write dynamic code.

Variables: The Data Holders

Imagine variables as containers that hold different types of information within your program. In PHP, you create a variable by using a dollar sign ($) followed by the variable name.

PHP

```
$name = "Alice";
$age = 30;
$price = 19.99;
```

PHP supports various data types, including:

Integers: Whole numbers (e.g., 10, -5, 0)

Floats: Decimal numbers (e.g., 3.14, -2.5)

Strings: Text enclosed in single or double quotes (e.g., "Hello", 'World')

Booleans: True or False values

Arrays: Ordered collections of values

Objects: Instances of classes (more on this later)

Operators: The Manipulators

Operators are symbols that perform actions on data. PHP offers a variety of operators, including:

Arithmetic Operators: +, -, *, /, % (modulo)

Assignment Operators: =, +=, -=, *=, /=, %=

Comparison Operators: == (equal), != (not equal), > (greater than), < (less than), >= (greater than or equal to), <= (less than or equal to)

Logical[1] Operators: and, or, xor, ! (not)

String Operators: . (concatenation)

Control Flow: Directing the Program's Path

Control flow statements determine the order in which your code is executed. They allow you to create dynamic programs that respond to different conditions.

Conditional Statements:

`if`: Executes a block of code if a condition is true.

`else`: Executes a block of code if the preceding `if` condition is false.

`elseif`: Specifies additional conditions to check.

`switch`: Selects one of many code blocks to execute based on the value of an expression.

PHP

```php
$age = 20;

if ($age >= 18) {
  echo "You are an adult.";
} else {
  echo "You are a minor.";
}
```

Loops:

`for`: Repeats a block of code a specific number of times.

`while`: Repeats a block of code as long as a condition is true.

`do...while`: Similar to `while`, but the code block is executed at least once.

`foreach`: Iterates over elements in an array.

PHP

```php
for ($i = 0; $i < 5; $i++) {
  echo $i . " ";
}
```

Functions: Reusable Code Blocks

Functions are named blocks of code that perform specific tasks. They help you organize your code and avoid repetition.

PHP

```php
function greet($name) {
  echo "Hello, " . $name . "!";
}

greet("Alice"); // Outputs "Hello, Alice!"
```

By mastering these core syntax and constructs, you'll gain a solid foundation in PHP programming. You'll be able to write dynamic code that manipulates data, responds to conditions, and performs complex tasks. This knowledge will serve as your bedrock as you progress to more advanced topics in web development.

Chapter 2

Mastering MySQL

2.1 Relational Databases and SQL Fundamentals

In the realm of web development, data is king. To effectively manage and utilize this valuable asset, we turn to relational databases – structured systems that organize data into interconnected tables. This chapter introduces you to the core concepts of relational databases and the language that governs them: SQL (Structured Query Language).

1. The Relational Model

Imagine a well-organized spreadsheet where data is arranged in rows and columns. This is the essence of a relational database. Data is stored in tables, where each row represents a record and each column represents a field. Relationships between tables are established through common fields, allowing for efficient data retrieval and manipulation.

2. Tables: The Building Blocks

A table is a collection of related data organized into rows and columns. Each table has a unique name and a defined structure, specifying the data type for each column. For example, a "customers" table might have columns for "customer_id," "name," "email," and "address."

3. Keys and Relationships

Keys are special fields that uniquely identify records within a table or establish relationships between tables.

Primary Key: Uniquely identifies each record in a table (e.g., "customer_id" in the "customers" table).

Foreign Key: References the primary key of another table, creating a link between the two (e.g., "customer_id" in an "orders" table referencing the "customers" table).

4. SQL: The Language of Databases

SQL is a powerful language used to communicate with relational databases. It provides a standardized way to perform various operations on data, including:

Creating Databases and Tables: CREATE DATABASE, CREATE TABLE

Inserting Data: INSERT INTO

Retrieving Data: SELECT

Updating Data: UPDATE

Deleting Data: DELETE

5. Basic SQL Queries

Let's explore some fundamental SQL queries:

Retrieving all data from a table:

SQL

```
SELECT * FROM customers;
```

Retrieving specific columns:

SQL

```
SELECT name, email FROM customers;
```

Filtering data with WHERE clause:

SQL

```
SELECT * FROM customers WHERE age > 25;
```

Sorting data with ORDER BY clause:

SQL

```
SELECT * FROM customers ORDER BY name ASC;
```

6. Data Integrity and Constraints

SQL provides mechanisms to ensure data integrity and enforce rules within your database.

NOT NULL: Ensures a column cannot have a null value.

UNIQUE: Ensures all values in a column are unique.

PRIMARY KEY: Combines NOT NULL and UNIQUE to uniquely identify each record.

FOREIGN KEY: Ensures referential integrity between tables.

7. Database Design Principles

Effective database design is crucial for efficient data management. Consider these principles:

Normalization: Reduces data redundancy and improves data integrity.

Data Types: Choose appropriate data types for each column to optimize storage and performance.

Indexing: Creates indexes on frequently accessed columns to speed up data retrieval.

By understanding these relational database and SQL fundamentals, you'll be well-equipped to design, manage, and interact with databases, a crucial skill for any web developer. As you delve deeper into SQL, you'll discover its power to perform complex queries, manipulate data, and unlock valuable insights.

2.2 Designing Efficient Database Schemas

A well-designed database schema is the backbone of any successful web application. It ensures data integrity, optimizes performance, and facilitates efficient data retrieval. This chapter dives into the principles and best practices for crafting database schemas that stand the test of time and scale with your application's needs.

1. Understanding the Requirements

Before you start sketching out tables and relationships, take the time to thoroughly understand the data your application will handle.

Identify Entities: What are the key objects or concepts you need to store information about? (e.g., users, products, orders)

Define Attributes: What characteristics or properties describe each entity? (e.g., user's name, email, product's price, order date)

Determine Relationships: How do these entities relate to each other? (e.g., a user can place many orders, a product can belong to multiple categories)

2. Normalization: The Path to Efficiency

Normalization is a process of organizing data to minimize redundancy and dependency issues. It involves breaking down large tables into smaller, more focused ones, connected through relationships.

First Normal Form (1NF): Eliminate repeating groups of data within a single table.

Second Normal Form (2NF): Remove redundant data that depends on only part of the primary key.

Third Normal Form (3NF): Eliminate data that depends on non-key attributes.

While normalization is crucial, excessive normalization can lead to an overabundance of tables and complex joins, potentially impacting performance. Strive for a balance that suits your application's specific needs.

3. Choosing Data Types Wisely

Selecting appropriate data types for each column is vital for storage efficiency and data integrity.

Numeric Types: `INT`, `DECIMAL`, `FLOAT` for storing numbers.

String Types: `VARCHAR`, `TEXT` for storing text data.

Date and Time Types: `DATE`, `TIME`, `DATETIME` for storing temporal information.

Boolean Type: `BOOLEAN` for storing true/false values.

Enum Type: `ENUM` for restricting a column to a predefined set of values.

4. Primary and Foreign Keys: Establishing Relationships

Primary keys uniquely identify records within a table, while foreign keys create links between tables.

Primary Key: Choose a column or a combination of columns that guarantees uniqueness (e.g., `user_id` in a `users` table).

Foreign Key: Reference the primary key of the related table to establish a connection (e.g., `customer_id` in an `orders` table referencing the `customers` table).

5. Indexing for Performance

Indexes are like lookup tables that speed up data retrieval. Create indexes on columns frequently used in `WHERE` clauses or join operations.

Single-Column Index: Indexes a single column.

Composite Index: Indexes multiple columns for more specific queries.

Unique Index: Ensures all values in the indexed column are unique.

6. Constraints for Data Integrity

Constraints enforce rules within your database to maintain data integrity.

NOT NULL: Ensures a column cannot have a null value.

UNIQUE: Ensures all values in a column are unique.

CHECK: Enforces specific conditions on data values.

DEFAULT: Provides a default value for a column if no value is specified.

7. Naming Conventions and Documentation

Adopt clear and consistent naming conventions for tables and columns. Use descriptive names that reflect the data they hold. Document your schema with comments to explain the purpose of tables, columns, and relationships.

8. Visualizing the Schema

Use database design tools or ER (Entity-Relationship) diagrams to visualize your schema. This helps identify potential issues and communicate the design to others.

By following these principles and best practices, you'll design efficient database schemas that provide a solid foundation for your web applications. Remember that database design is an iterative process. As your application evolves, your schema may need adjustments to accommodate new requirements and optimize performance.

2.3 Working with Data: CRUD Operations and Beyond

Now that you understand the foundations of relational databases and SQL, it's time to roll up your sleeves and start working with data. This chapter explores the fundamental CRUD operations – Create, Read, Update, and Delete – the cornerstones of data manipulation in web applications.

1. Creating Data (C)

The `INSERT INTO` statement is your tool for adding new records to a table. It specifies the table name and the values to be inserted for each column.

SQL

```
INSERT INTO customers (name, email, age)

 VALUES ('John Doe', 'john.doe@example.com',
30);
```

2. Reading Data (R)

The SELECT statement is your key to retrieving data from a table. It allows you to specify the columns you want to retrieve, filter data based on conditions, and sort the results.

SQL

```
-- Retrieve all columns from the 'customers'
table

SELECT * FROM customers;



-- Retrieve specific columns

SELECT name, email FROM customers;



-- Filter data using a WHERE clause

SELECT * FROM customers WHERE age > 25;



-- Sort results using an ORDER BY clause
```

```
SELECT * FROM customers ORDER BY name ASC;
```

3. Updating Data (U)

The `UPDATE` statement modifies existing records in a table. It allows you to specify the columns to be updated and the new values, along with a `WHERE` clause to target specific rows.

SQL

```
UPDATE customers

SET email = 'john.updated@example.com'

WHERE customer_id = 1;
```

4. Deleting Data (D)

The `DELETE` statement removes records from a table. Use a `WHERE` clause to specify the rows to be deleted.

SQL

```
DELETE FROM customers WHERE customer_id = 1;
```

5. Beyond CRUD: Advanced SQL

While CRUD operations form the foundation of data manipulation, SQL offers a wealth of advanced features to perform more complex tasks.

Aggregate Functions: `COUNT`, `SUM`, `AVG`, `MAX`, `MIN` to calculate summary statistics.

JOIN Operations: Combine data from multiple tables based on related columns.

Subqueries: Embed queries within other queries for more complex filtering and retrieval.

Transactions: Group multiple SQL statements into a single unit of work to ensure data consistency.

Stored Procedures: Pre-compiled SQL code that can be reused for common tasks.

6. Data Validation and Sanitization

Before performing any CRUD operation, validate and sanitize user input to prevent errors and security vulnerabilities like SQL injection.

Data Type Validation: Ensure data matches the expected type for each column.

Input Sanitization: Remove or escape special characters that could interfere with SQL queries.

7. Error Handling

Implement error handling to gracefully handle potential issues during data operations. Use try-catch blocks to catch exceptions and provide informative error messages.

By mastering CRUD operations and exploring the advanced capabilities of SQL, you'll gain the skills to effectively manage and manipulate data in your web applications. As you continue your journey, you'll discover the power of SQL to unlock valuable insights and build dynamic, data-driven experiences.

Chapter 3

Connecting PHP & MySQL

3.1   Establishing   Secure   Database Connections with PDO

Connecting to your database is the crucial first step in any PHP and MySQL application. But it's not just about establishing a connection; it's about doing so securely. This chapter introduces you to PDO (PHP Data Objects), a powerful and secure way to interact with your MySQL database.

1. Why PDO?

PDO offers several advantages over older database connection methods like `mysql_connect`:

Security: PDO provides prepared statements, a powerful tool to prevent SQL injection attacks.

Portability: PDO supports multiple database systems, making it easy to switch between different databases if needed.

Object-Oriented Interface: PDO provides a clean and consistent object-oriented API for database operations.

Error Handling: PDO uses exceptions for error handling, allowing for more robust error management.

2. Connecting to the Database

To establish a connection using PDO, you need to create a new PDO instance with the necessary connection parameters:

PHP

```php
try {

  $host = 'localhost';

  $dbname = 'your_database_name';

  $username = 'your_username';

  $password = 'your_password';



              $pdo              =              new
PDO("mysql:host=$host;dbname=$dbname", $username,
$password);

  // Set PDO error mode to exception

           $pdo->setAttribute(PDO::ATTR_ERRMODE,
PDO::ERRMODE_EXCEPTION);[1]

  echo "Connected successfully!";

} catch(PDOException $e) {

  echo "Connection failed: " . $e->getMessage();[2]

}
```

In this code:

We create a new PDO object, providing the database driver (`mysql`), host, database name, username, and password.

We set the error mode to `PDO::ERRMODE_EXCEPTION` to ensure that any database errors will throw exceptions, allowing for better error handling.

3. Prepared Statements: Shielding Against SQL Injection

Prepared statements are a vital security measure that separate SQL code from user-supplied data, effectively preventing SQL injection attacks.

PHP

```php
$stmt = $pdo->prepare("SELECT * FROM users WHERE username = :username AND password = :password");

$stmt->bindParam(':username', $username);

$stmt->bindParam(':password', $password);

$stmt->execute();[3]
```

Here's how it works:

The SQL query is prepared with placeholders (`:username`, `:password`).

The `bindParam` method binds these placeholders to variables, ensuring that user input is treated as data, not executable code.

The `execute` method executes the prepared statement with the bound values.

4. Fetching Data

After executing a query, you can retrieve the results using different fetch methods:

`fetch()`: Fetches a single row as an object or an array.

`fetchAll()`: Fetches all rows as an array of objects or arrays.

PHP

```php
$stmt = $pdo->query("SELECT * FROM users");

while ($row = $stmt->fetch(PDO::FETCH_ASSOC)) {

    echo $row['name'] . "<br>";

}
```

5. Error Handling and Security

Displaying Errors: In a development environment, it's helpful to display error messages to identify issues. However, in a production environment, avoid exposing sensitive information in error messages.

Storing Credentials: Store your database credentials securely, preferably outside of your web root directory, and avoid hardcoding them directly in your code. Consider using environment variables or configuration files.

6. Closing the Connection

Although PHP automatically closes the connection when the script ends, it's good practice to explicitly close it using `$pdo = null;` when you're finished with database operations.

By adopting PDO and utilizing prepared statements, you can establish secure and reliable database connections, safeguarding your application against SQL injection and ensuring the integrity of your data.

3.2 Executing Queries and Fetching Results

Once you've established a secure connection to your MySQL database using PDO, the next step is to execute SQL queries and retrieve the results. This chapter explores the various methods PDO provides for interacting with your database and processing the data it returns.

1. Executing Queries

PDO offers two primary methods for executing SQL queries:

`exec()`: Use this method for queries that don't return a result set, such as `INSERT`, `UPDATE`, and `DELETE` statements. It returns the number of rows affected by the query.

PHP

```php
$sql = "INSERT INTO users (name, email) VALUES
('Alice', 'alice@example.com')";

$affectedRows = $pdo->exec($sql);

echo "Number of rows inserted: " . $affectedRows;
```

`query()`: Use this method for queries that return a result set, such as `SELECT` statements. It returns a PDOStatement object, which represents the result set.

PHP

```php
$stmt = $pdo->query("SELECT * FROM users");
```

2. Fetching Results

After executing a `SELECT` query using `query()`, you can retrieve the results using various fetch methods:

`fetch()`: This method fetches a single row from the result set. You can specify the fetch mode to determine how the data is returned (e.g., as an associative array, an indexed array, or an object).

PHP

```php
$row = $stmt->fetch(PDO::FETCH_ASSOC); // Fetch as associative array

echo $row['name'];
```

`fetchAll()`: This method fetches all rows from the result set and returns them as an array. You can also specify the fetch mode here.

PHP

```php
$rows = $stmt->fetchAll(PDO::FETCH_ASSOC);

foreach ($rows as $row) {

  echo $row['name'] . "<br>";

}
```

3. Fetch Modes

PDO offers several fetch modes to control how the data is returned:

PDO::FETCH_ASSOC: Returns an associative array, where the column names are the keys.

PDO::FETCH_NUM: Returns an indexed array, where the column values are indexed numerically.

PDO::FETCH_OBJ: Returns an object, where the column names are the object properties.

PDO::FETCH_BOTH: Returns an array that combines both PDO::FETCH_ASSOC and PDO::FETCH_NUM.

4. Binding Parameters in query()

While query() is typically used for SELECT statements, you can also use it with parameterized queries for added security.

PHP

```php
$stmt = $pdo->query("SELECT * FROM users WHERE id = " . $_GET['id']); // Vulnerable to SQL injection
```

```php
// Secure way using parameterized query

$stmt = $pdo->prepare("SELECT * FROM users WHERE
id = :id");

$stmt->bindParam(':id', $_GET['id']);

  $stmt->execute();
```

5. Iterating Through Results

You can iterate through the result set using a `while` loop and the `fetch()` method:

PHP

```php
while ($row = $stmt->fetch(PDO::FETCH_ASSOC)) {

  // Process each row here

}
```

Or, you can use a `foreach` loop with `fetchAll()`:

PHP

```php
foreach    ($stmt->fetchAll(PDO::FETCH_ASSOC)    as
$row) {

  // Process each row here
```

```
}
```

6. Closing the Cursor

After fetching the results, it's good practice to close the cursor using `$stmt->closeCursor();` to release the database resources.

By mastering these techniques for executing queries and fetching results, you'll be well-equipped to interact with your MySQL database and retrieve the data you need to power your web applications. Remember to always prioritize security by using prepared statements or parameterized queries to prevent SQL injection vulnerabilities.

3.3 Preventing SQL Injection Vulnerabilities

SQL injection is a serious security threat that can compromise your entire web application. It occurs when malicious SQL code is inserted into user input, allowing attackers to manipulate your database and potentially steal sensitive data. This chapter equips you with the knowledge and techniques to effectively prevent SQL injection vulnerabilities.

1. Understanding the Threat

Imagine a login form where a user enters their username and password. An attacker could enter a malicious SQL query into the username field, such as:

SQL

```
'  OR  '1'='1
```

If this input is directly concatenated into an SQL query, it could bypass authentication and grant the attacker access to the entire database.

2. Prepared Statements: The First Line of Defense

Prepared statements are your primary weapon against SQL injection. They separate SQL code from user-supplied data, ensuring that user input is treated as data, not executable code.

PHP

```php
$stmt = $pdo->prepare("SELECT * FROM users WHERE username = :username AND password = :password");

$stmt->bindParam(':username', $username);

$stmt->bindParam(':password', $password);

$stmt->execute();[1]
```

By using placeholders (:username, :password) and binding parameters, you prevent malicious SQL code from being injected into your query.

3. Parameterized Queries

Even when using methods like query(), you can still incorporate parameterization for added security.

PHP

```php
$stmt = $pdo->prepare("SELECT * FROM users WHERE
id = :id");

$stmt->bindParam(':id', $_GET['id']);

$stmt->execute();
```

This approach ensures that user input from `$_GET['id']` is treated as a value, not as part of the SQL query.

4. Input Validation and Sanitization

While prepared statements are crucial, input validation and sanitization add an extra layer of protection.

Validate Data Types: Ensure that user input matches the expected data type for each column (e.g., integer, string, date).

Sanitize Input: Remove or escape special characters that could interfere with SQL queries. Use functions like `htmlspecialchars()` to encode HTML entities and prevent cross-site scripting (XSS) attacks.

5. Least Privilege Principle

Grant database users only the necessary privileges to perform their tasks. Avoid using the root user for your web application. Create separate users with limited permissions to minimize the potential damage from an attack.

6. Database Firewalls

Consider using a database firewall to monitor and block suspicious activity, such as SQL injection attempts. These firewalls can analyze incoming SQL traffic and identify patterns that indicate malicious intent.

7. Regular Security Audits

Conduct regular security audits of your code and database configuration to identify and address potential vulnerabilities. Use automated tools and manual code reviews to ensure your application remains secure.

8. Stay Informed

Keep up-to-date with the latest security best practices and vulnerabilities. Follow security blogs, attend conferences, and participate in online communities to stay informed about emerging threats and mitigation strategies.

By diligently applying these preventive measures, you can significantly reduce the risk of SQL injection vulnerabilities and protect your web application and its valuable data. Remember that security is an ongoing process, requiring continuous vigilance and adaptation to evolving threats.

Chapter 4

Object-Oriented PHP for Web Development

4.1 Classes, Objects, and Inheritance: Building Reusable Code

Object-Oriented Programming (OOP) is a powerful paradigm that allows you to structure your code in a more organized, modular, and reusable way. This chapter introduces you to the core concepts of OOP in PHP: classes, objects, and inheritance.

1. Classes: The Blueprints

Think of a class as a blueprint for creating objects. It defines a structure that encapsulates data (properties) and actions (methods) that operate on that data.

PHP

```php
class User {

  // Properties

  public $name;

  public $email;



  // Methods
```

```php
    public function greet() {

        return "Hello, my name is " . $this->name;

    }

}
```

In this example, we define a `User` class with properties `$name` and `$email` and a method `greet()`.

2. Objects: The Instances

An object is an instance of a class. It's like creating a specific user from the `User` blueprint.

PHP

```php
$user1 = new User();

$user1->name = "Alice";

$user1->email = "alice@example.com";

echo $user1->greet(); // Outputs "Hello, my name is Alice"
```

Here, `$user1` is an object of the `User` class. We assign values to its properties and call its `greet()` method.

3. Inheritance: Extending Functionality

Inheritance allows you to create new classes (child classes) that inherit properties and methods from existing classes (parent classes). This promotes code reuse and allows you to create a hierarchy of classes.

PHP

```php
class Admin extends User {

  // Additional property

  public $isAdmin = true;



  // Overriding the greet() method

  public function greet() {

    return "Hello, I'm admin " . $this->name;

  }

}



$admin1 = new Admin();

$admin1->name = "Bob";

echo $admin1->greet(); // Outputs "Hello, I'm admin Bob"
```

The `Admin` class inherits from the `User` class, adding an `$isAdmin` property and overriding the `greet()` method.

4. Access Modifiers

Access modifiers control the visibility of properties and methods:

`public`: Accessible from anywhere.

`protected`: Accessible within the class and its subclasses.

`private`: Accessible only within the class.

5. Constructors

Constructors are special methods that are automatically called when an object is created. They are used to initialize properties.

PHP

```php
class User {

  public $name;

  public $email;


  public function __construct($name, $email) {

    $this->name = $name;

    $this->email = $email;
```

```
    }

}


$user1 = new User("Alice", "alice@example.com");
```

6. Benefits of OOP

Code Reusability: Inheritance allows you to reuse code and avoid redundancy.

Modularity: Classes encapsulate data and actions, making code more organized and maintainable.

Flexibility: OOP allows for easy modification and extension of code.

Encapsulation: Protects data by controlling access to it through methods.

By understanding these OOP concepts, you can write more structured, efficient, and reusable code for your PHP web applications. As you delve deeper into OOP, you'll discover more advanced features like interfaces, abstract classes, and polymorphism, which further enhance the power and flexibility of your code.

4.2 Design Patterns for Web Applications

Design patterns are reusable solutions to common problems in software design. They provide proven approaches to structuring your code, making it more maintainable, scalable, and efficient.

This chapter explores some essential design patterns commonly used in web development.

1. Model-View-Controller (MVC)

MVC is a foundational pattern that separates an application into three interconnected components:

Model: Represents the data and business logic of the application.

View: Displays the data to the[1] user and handles user interaction.

Controller: Acts as an intermediary between the Model and View, handling user requests and updating the Model accordingly.

MVC promotes code organization, reusability, and separation of concerns, making it easier to develop, test, and maintain web applications.

2. Front Controller

The Front Controller pattern provides a centralized entry point for handling all incoming requests. It acts as a "traffic cop," directing requests to the appropriate controllers and actions. This pattern simplifies request handling, promotes code reuse, and allows for centralized implementation of security and logging.

3. Dependency Injection

Dependency Injection is a technique for decoupling objects by providing their dependencies from external sources rather than having them create those dependencies themselves. This promotes code reusability, testability, and maintainability by reducing tight coupling between objects.

4. Repository Pattern

The Repository pattern provides an abstraction layer between the data access logic and the rest of the application. It defines a clear interface for accessing data, allowing you to easily switch between different data sources or persistence mechanisms without affecting the rest of your code.

5. Middleware

Middleware acts as a series of filters or layers that process requests before they reach the final handler. It can be used for various tasks like authentication, authorization, logging, and input validation. Middleware promotes code modularity and allows you to easily add or remove functionality without modifying core application code.

6. Template Method

The Template Method pattern defines a skeleton of an algorithm in an operation, deferring some steps to subclasses. This allows subclasses to redefine certain steps of an algorithm without changing the algorithm's structure.[2]

7. Singleton

The Singleton pattern ensures that a class has only one instance and provides a global point of access to it. This is useful for managing[3] shared resources or providing a single point of control for certain functionalities.

8. Observer

The Observer pattern defines a one-to-many dependency between objects so that when one object changes state, all its dependents are notified and[4] updated automatically. This is useful for implementing event-driven[5] systems and keeping different parts of your application synchronized.

9. Strategy

The Strategy pattern defines a family of algorithms, encapsulates each one, and makes them interchangeable. This allows[6] you to select different algorithms at runtime based on specific needs.

10. Factory Method

The Factory Method pattern defines an interface for creating objects but lets subclasses decide which class to instantiate. This pattern promotes loose coupling[7] by deferring instantiation to subclasses.

By understanding and applying these design patterns, you can significantly improve the design and architecture of your web applications. They provide proven solutions to common challenges, promoting code reusability, maintainability, and scalability. As you gain more experience, you'll discover even more design patterns and learn how to effectively incorporate them into your development process.

4.3 Leveraging Frameworks: Introduction to Laravel

While you can build web applications from scratch using raw PHP and MySQL, leveraging a framework can significantly streamline the development process, enhance code organization, and improve security. This chapter introduces you to Laravel, a popular PHP framework known for its elegant syntax, developer-friendly features, and robust ecosystem.

1. Why Laravel?

Laravel offers numerous benefits that make it a compelling choice for web development:

Elegant Syntax: Laravel's expressive and intuitive syntax makes writing code a joy. It simplifies common tasks and reduces boilerplate code, allowing you to focus on building your application's unique features.

MVC Architecture: Laravel follows the Model-View-Controller (MVC) architectural pattern, promoting code organization and separation of concerns. This makes your application more maintainable and testable.

Artisan CLI: Laravel's command-line interface (CLI), Artisan, provides a powerful tool for automating tasks, generating code, and managing database migrations.

Eloquent ORM: Eloquent is Laravel's Object-Relational Mapper (ORM) that provides a beautiful, simple ActiveRecord implementation for working with your database. It allows you to interact with your database[1] using expressive PHP syntax instead of writing raw SQL queries.

Blade Templating Engine: Blade is a powerful and intuitive templating engine that allows you to create dynamic views with ease. It supports template inheritance, layouts, and convenient syntax for common tasks.

Robust Ecosystem: Laravel boasts a rich ecosystem of packages and tools that extend its functionality. This includes packages for authentication, authorization, API development, testing, and more.

Active Community: Laravel has a large and vibrant community of developers, providing ample resources, support, and contributions to the framework.

2. Getting Started with Laravel

To begin your Laravel journey, you'll need to install it on your development environment. You can use Composer, a PHP dependency manager, to install Laravel:

Bash

```
composer         create-project         --prefer-dist
laravel/laravel your-project-name
```

This command will create a new Laravel project in a directory named "your-project-name."

3. Exploring the Laravel Structure

Once installed, familiarize yourself with the key directories and files in a Laravel project:

app: Contains the core code of your application, including models, controllers, and middleware.

config: Holds configuration files for your application.

database: Contains database migrations and seeders.

public: The web root directory, containing the index.php file and your assets (CSS, JavaScript, images).

resources: Holds your views (Blade templates) and language files.

routes: Defines the routes for your application.

4. Building a Simple Application

Let's create a simple web page that displays "Hello, World!" using Laravel:

1 Define a Route: In `routes/web.php`, add the following route:

PHP

```php
Route::get('/', function () {

  return view('welcome');

});
```

This route maps the root URL ("/") to a closure that returns the `welcome` view.

2 Create a View: In `resources/views`, create a file named `welcome.blade.php` and add the following code:

HTML

```html
<!DOCTYPE html>

<html>

<head>

  <title>Welcome to Laravel</title>

</head>

<body>

  <h1>Hello, World!</h1>

</body>
```

```
</html>
```

3 Start the Development Server: Run the following command in your terminal:

Bash

```
php artisan serve
```

This will start a development server. Open your browser and visit `http://localhost:8000` to see your "Hello, World!" message.

5. Next Steps

This is just a glimpse into the power of Laravel. As you delve deeper, you'll explore:

Database interactions with Eloquent: Creating models, performing CRUD operations, and defining relationships.

Building controllers and actions: Handling user requests, processing data, and returning responses.

Creating dynamic views with Blade: Designing layouts, using template inheritance, and displaying data.

Utilizing Artisan commands: Generating code, managing databases, and running tests.

Leveraging the Laravel ecosystem: Exploring packages for authentication, API development, and more.

By mastering Laravel, you'll gain a powerful tool for building modern, robust, and scalable web applications. Its elegant syntax, rich features, and active community make it a compelling choice for developers of all levels.

Chapter 5

User Interface Design with HTML, CSS & JavaScript

5.1 Modern HTML5 and CSS3 for Dynamic Layouts

Gone are the days of static, rigid web pages. Modern web design demands dynamic layouts that adapt seamlessly to different screen sizes and devices. This chapter explores the powerful features of HTML5 and CSS3 that empower you to create responsive, visually engaging, and user-friendly web experiences.

1. HTML5 Structural Elements

HTML5 introduced a set of semantic elements that provide meaning and structure to your web content. These elements not only improve code readability but also enhance accessibility and SEO.

`<header>`: Defines the header section of a page or section.

`<nav>`: Represents a section with navigation links.

`<main>`: Specifies the main content of a document.

`<article>`: Represents a self-contained composition in a document, page, application, or site.

`<aside>`: Defines content aside from the main content (e.g., a sidebar).

`<footer>`: Defines the footer section of a page or section.

By using these elements, you create a well-structured document that is easier to understand for both browsers and assistive technologies.

2. CSS3 Flexible Box Layout (Flexbox)

Flexbox is a powerful CSS3 layout module that provides a flexible way to arrange items within a container. It simplifies tasks like horizontal and vertical alignment, distribution of space, and reordering of elements.

`display: flex;`: Enables flexbox layout for a container.

`flex-direction`: Specifies the direction of the flex container's main axis (row or column).

`justify-content`: Aligns items along the main axis (e.g., center, space-between, space-around).

`align-items`: Aligns items along the cross axis (e.g., center, flex-start, flex-end).

`flex-wrap`: Controls whether the flex items should wrap or not.

Flexbox provides a powerful and intuitive way to create dynamic layouts that adapt to different screen sizes and content variations.

3. CSS3 Grid Layout

Grid Layout is another powerful CSS3 module that allows you to create two-dimensional grid-based layouts. It provides a flexible and robust way to arrange items in rows and columns, offering fine-grained control over layout structure.

`display: grid;`: Enables grid layout for a container.

`grid-template-columns`: Defines the number and width of columns in the grid.

`grid-template-rows`: Defines the number and height of rows in the grid.

`grid-gap`: Specifies the spacing between grid rows and columns.

`grid-template-areas`: Names grid areas and assigns grid items to them.

Grid Layout excels in creating complex, multi-column layouts and provides a powerful tool for responsive design.

4. Media Queries for Responsiveness

Media queries allow you to apply different styles based on device characteristics, such as screen size, resolution, and orientation. This is essential for creating responsive layouts that adapt to various devices.

CSS

```css
@media (max-width: 768px) {

  /* Styles for screens smaller than 768px */

  .container {

    width: 90%;

  }

}
```

By using media queries, you can tailor your layout and styles to provide an optimal viewing experience across a wide range of devices.

5. CSS3 Transitions and Animations

CSS3 transitions and animations add dynamic visual effects to your web pages, enhancing user engagement and interactivity.

Transitions: Create smooth transitions between different states of an element (e.g., hover effects, changes in color or size).

Animations: Allow you to create more complex animations with keyframes, defining the start and end states of an animation.

These features enable you to add subtle animations or create visually striking effects, enhancing the overall user experience.

6. Other CSS3 Features

CSS3 offers a plethora of other features that enhance your design capabilities:

Transforms: Rotate, scale, skew, or translate elements in 2D or 3D space.

Gradients: Create smooth transitions between colors.

Shadows: Add depth and dimension to elements.

Rounded Corners: Create rounded corners without images.

Background Images: Control background image size, position, and repetition.

By mastering these modern HTML5 and CSS3 techniques, you'll be well-equipped to create dynamic, responsive, and visually engaging web layouts that provide an optimal user experience across a wide range of devices.

5.2 Interactive User Experiences with JavaScript

While HTML provides the structure and CSS styles your web page, JavaScript is the magic that brings it to life. It enables you to create dynamic and interactive elements that respond to user actions, enhancing the overall user experience. This chapter explores the power of JavaScript in crafting engaging and user-friendly web interfaces.

1. Event Handling: Responding to User Actions

JavaScript allows you to capture and respond to various events that occur on a web page, such as mouse clicks, keyboard input, and page loads. This is achieved through event listeners that trigger specific JavaScript code when a particular event happens.

JavaScript

```
// Add an event listener to a button

const button = document.getElementById('myButton');

button.addEventListener('click', function() {

  alert('Button clicked!');[1]

});
```

This code snippet demonstrates how to add a click event listener to a button, triggering an alert message when the button is clicked.

2. DOM Manipulation: Dynamic Content Updates

The Document Object Model (DOM) represents the structure of an HTML document. JavaScript can manipulate the DOM to dynamically[2] update content, modify styles, and add or remove elements.

JavaScript

```
// Change the text content of an element

const heading = document.getElementById('myHeading');

heading.textContent = 'New Heading';



// Add a new paragraph to the page

const paragraph = document.createElement('p');

paragraph.textContent = 'This is a new paragraph.';

document.body.appendChild(paragraph);[3]
```

This code showcases how to change the text content of a heading and add a new paragraph to the page using JavaScript.

3. Form Validation: Ensuring Data Integrity

JavaScript plays a crucial role in form validation, ensuring that users provide valid and complete information before submitting a form. This prevents errors and improves data integrity.

JavaScript

```
// Validate an email field

const                    emailInput              =
document.getElementById('email');

emailInput.addEventListener('blur', function() {

  if (!validateEmail(emailInput.value)) {

    alert('Please enter a valid email address.');

  }

});
```

This example demonstrates how to validate an email field when it loses focus, ensuring that the user enters a valid email address.

4. AJAX: Seamless Data Fetching

AJAX (Asynchronous JavaScript and XML) allows you to fetch data from a server without reloading the entire page. This enables you to create dynamic and responsive web applications that update content seamlessly.

JavaScript

```javascript
// Fetch data from a server using AJAX

const xhr = new XMLHttpRequest();

xhr.open('GET', 'data.json');

xhr.onload = function() {

  if (xhr.status === 200) {

    const data = JSON.parse(xhr.responseText);

    // Process the fetched data

  }

};

xhr.send();
```

This code snippet shows how to fetch data from a JSON file using AJAX and process it once the request is successful.

5. Animations and Visual Effects

JavaScript can create animations and visual effects that enhance user engagement and interactivity. You can animate elements, create transitions, and add dynamic visual feedback to user actions.

6. User Interface Libraries and Frameworks

JavaScript UI libraries and frameworks like React, Angular, and Vue.js provide pre-built components and tools that simplify the development of complex user interfaces. They offer features like data binding, component-based architecture, and state management, making it easier to create interactive and dynamic web applications.

By mastering these JavaScript techniques, you can create interactive and engaging user experiences that enhance the functionality and appeal of your web applications. JavaScript empowers you to build dynamic interfaces, respond to user actions, and create seamless web experiences that captivate your audience.

5.3 Integrating Front-End and Back-End Code

In modern web development, the seamless integration of front-end and back-end code is crucial for creating dynamic, interactive, and user-friendly applications. This chapter explores the key concepts and techniques for connecting your front-end (HTML, CSS, JavaScript) with your back-end (PHP, MySQL) to build cohesive and functional web experiences.

1. The Role of APIs

APIs (Application Programming Interfaces) act as the bridge between your front-end and back-end. They define a set of rules and specifications that allow these two layers to communicate and exchange data. RESTful APIs are a popular architectural style for building web APIs, relying on HTTP methods (GET, POST, PUT, DELETE) to perform actions and exchange data in formats like JSON or XML.

2. Front-End Communication with AJAX

AJAX (Asynchronous JavaScript and XML) enables your front-end to communicate with the back-end without requiring a full page reload. This allows for dynamic content updates and a more responsive user experience.

JavaScript

```
// Example using Fetch API

fetch('/api/users')

  .then(response => response.json())

  .then(users => {

    // Process the fetched user data

  });
```

This code snippet demonstrates how to fetch user data from a back-end API endpoint using the Fetch API.

3. Back-End Handling of Requests

Your back-end code, written in PHP, handles API requests from the front-end. It processes the requests, interacts with the database (MySQL), and sends back the appropriate responses.

PHP

```
// Example using a PHP framework like Laravel
```

```
Route::get('/api/users', function () {

  $users = User::all();

  return response()->json($users);

});
```

This example shows a simple route in Laravel that fetches all users from the database and returns them as a JSON response.

4. Data Exchange Formats

JSON (JavaScript Object Notation) is a popular data exchange format due to its lightweight nature and compatibility with JavaScript. Your back-end encodes data into JSON format, and your front-end parses this JSON data to display it or use it for further processing.

5. Security Considerations

When integrating front-end and back-end code, security is paramount.

Authentication: Implement robust authentication mechanisms to verify user identities and protect sensitive data.

Authorization: Control access to resources based on user roles and permissions.

Input Validation: Validate and sanitize all user input on both the front-end and back-end to prevent vulnerabilities like SQL injection and cross-site scripting (XSS).

HTTPS: Use HTTPS to encrypt communication between the front-end and back-end, protecting data in transit.

6. State Management

For complex web applications, consider using a state management library or framework (e.g., Redux, Vuex) to manage the application's state and data flow between the front-end and back-end.

7. Testing and Debugging

Thoroughly test your front-end and back-end integration to ensure seamless communication and data exchange. Use browser developer tools and debugging techniques to identify and resolve any issues.

By effectively integrating your front-end and back-end code, you can create dynamic, interactive, and user-friendly web applications. APIs, AJAX, and secure coding practices are essential tools in your arsenal for building cohesive and functional web experiences.

Chapter 6

User Authentication and Session Management

6.1 Secure Password Hashing and Storage

Protecting user passwords is a critical responsibility in web development. Storing passwords in plain text is a major security risk, leaving your users vulnerable to data breaches. This chapter delves into the essential techniques for secure password hashing and storage, ensuring that even if your database is compromised, the passwords remain protected.

1. Why Hashing?

Hashing is a one-way process that transforms a password into a unique, fixed-length string of characters. This makes it virtually impossible to reverse the process and recover the original password from the hash. Even if an attacker gains access to the hashed passwords, they cannot easily decipher them.

2. Choosing a Strong Hashing Algorithm

Selecting a robust hashing algorithm is crucial. Avoid outdated algorithms like MD5 or SHA1, as they are susceptible to attacks. Recommended options include:

bcrypt: A widely used and trusted algorithm that is computationally expensive, making it resistant to brute-force attacks.

Argon2: A more recent algorithm that is memory-intensive, making it even more challenging for attackers with specialized hardware.

scrypt: Another memory-hard algorithm that offers strong security.

3. Salting: Adding an Extra Layer of Protection

Salting involves adding a unique, random string of characters (the "salt") to the password before hashing it. This prevents attackers from using pre-computed tables (rainbow tables) to crack common passwords.

PHP

```php
$salt = random_bytes(16); // Generate a random salt

$hashedPassword = password_hash($password . $salt, PASSWORD_DEFAULT);
```

Store the salt along with the hashed password in your database.

4. Using Password Hashing APIs

Modern programming languages provide built-in functions or libraries for secure password hashing. Utilize these APIs to simplify the process and ensure you're using best practices.

PHP: `password_hash()` and `password_verify()`

Python: `bcrypt` library

Node.js: `bcrypt` or `scrypt` packages

5. Storing Hashes Securely

Even with strong hashing and salting, it's vital to store the password hashes securely.

Database Security: Implement strong database security measures, including access controls, encryption, and regular backups.

Separate Storage: Consider storing sensitive data like password hashes in a separate database or server to minimize the impact of a breach.

Limit Access: Grant database access only to authorized users and applications with the least privilege principle.

6. Password Strength and Complexity

Encourage users to create strong and unique passwords. Enforce password complexity rules (e.g., minimum length, combination of characters) and consider using password strength meters to provide feedback to users.

7. Other Security Measures

Two-Factor Authentication (2FA): Add an extra layer of security by requiring users to provide a second form of verification (e.g., code from a mobile app).

Password Reset Mechanisms: Implement secure password reset procedures that involve email verification or other security measures.

Regular Security Audits: Conduct regular security audits to identify and address any potential vulnerabilities in your password storage and handling practices.

By following these best practices for secure password hashing and storage, you can significantly enhance the security of your web application and protect your users' sensitive information. Remember that password security is an ongoing commitment, requiring continuous vigilance and adaptation to evolving threats.

6.2 Implementing User Login and Registration Systems

User authentication is a cornerstone of many web applications, allowing users to create accounts, securely log in, and access personalized features. This chapter guides you through the process of implementing user login and registration systems, ensuring secure and user-friendly authentication for your web application.

1. Registration System

Registration Form: Create a registration form that captures essential user information, such as username, email address, and password.

Input Validation: Implement client-side and server-side validation to ensure data integrity and prevent malicious input.

Password Hashing: Hash the password using a strong hashing algorithm (e.g., bcrypt, Argon2) and a unique salt to protect it even if your database is compromised.

Data Storage: Store the username, hashed password, and salt in your database. Consider adding fields for email verification status and user roles.

Email Verification: Send a verification email to the user's registered email address. Include a unique link that allows them to activate their account.

2. Login System

Login Form: Create a login form that prompts the user for their username or email address and password.

Authentication: Retrieve the user's record from the database based on their username or email.

Password Verification: Verify the entered password against the stored hashed password using `password_verify()` (in PHP) or an equivalent function in your chosen language.

Session Management: Upon successful authentication, create a new session for the user and store relevant information, such as their user ID and role.

Remember Me Functionality: Optionally, provide a "Remember Me" checkbox that allows users to stay logged in for an extended period using cookies.

3. Security Considerations

Password Complexity: Enforce strong password requirements (e.g., minimum length, character diversity) to encourage secure passwords.

Brute-Force Protection: Implement measures to prevent brute-force attacks, such as account lockouts after multiple failed login attempts.

Session Security: Secure your session management mechanism by using HTTPS, regenerating session IDs periodically, and setting appropriate cookie attributes (e.g., `HttpOnly`, `Secure`).

Two-Factor Authentication (2FA): Consider adding 2FA as an extra layer of security, requiring users to provide a second form of verification (e.g., code from a mobile app).

4. User Experience (UX)

Clear Error Messages: Provide informative error messages to guide users through the registration and login process.

Password Recovery: Implement a password recovery mechanism that allows users to reset their passwords securely.

Social Login: Consider integrating social login options (e.g., Google, Facebook) to simplify the registration and login process.

5. Code Example (PHP with PDO)

PHP

```php
// Login example

$stmt = $pdo->prepare("SELECT * FROM users WHERE username = :username");

$stmt->bindParam(':username', $username);

$stmt->execute();

$user = $stmt->fetch(PDO::FETCH_ASSOC);



if ($user[1] && password_verify($password, $user['password'])) {

  // Authentication successful

  $_SESSION['user_id'] = $user['id'];[2]

  // Redirect to user dashboard

} else {

  // Authentication failed

  // Display error message

}
```

By following these guidelines and prioritizing security, you can implement robust user login and registration systems that provide a secure and user-friendly authentication experience for your web application. Remember to stay updated with the latest security best practices and adapt your implementation to evolving threats.

6.3 Managing User Sessions and Permissions

Once a user logs in, you need a way to maintain their authenticated state and control their access to different parts of your application. This chapter explores how to manage user sessions and implement permission systems to ensure secure and personalized user experiences.

1. Session Management

Session Start: Initiate a session using `session_start()` (in PHP) or an equivalent function in your chosen language. This creates a unique session ID for the user and allows you to store session data.

Storing Session Data: Store relevant user information in the session, such as their user ID, username, and role.

PHP

```php
$_SESSION['user_id'] = $user['id'];

$_SESSION['username'] = $user['username'];

$_SESSION['role'] = $user['role'];
```

Accessing Session Data: Access session data across different pages to personalize the user experience and control access to features.

PHP

```php
if (isset($_SESSION['user_id'])) {

  // User is logged in

  echo "Welcome, " . $_SESSION['username'];

}
```

Session Timeout: Implement session timeouts to automatically log out inactive users after a certain period. This enhances security by preventing unauthorized access from unattended sessions.

Session Regeneration: Regenerate session IDs periodically to mitigate the risk of session hijacking.

Session Destruction: Destroy the session when the user logs out using `session_destroy()` or an equivalent function. This invalidates the session ID and removes associated data.

2. Permission Systems

Role-Based Access Control (RBAC): Assign roles to users (e.g., admin, editor, viewer) and define permissions associated with each role. This simplifies permission management and ensures consistent access control.

Access Control Lists (ACLs): For more fine-grained control, use ACLs to define specific permissions for individual users or groups.

Permission Checks: Implement checks within your code to verify if a user has the necessary permissions to access a particular resource or perform an action.

PHP

```php
if ($_SESSION['role'] === 'admin') {

  // Allow access to admin features

}
```

Database Design: Incorporate user roles and permissions into your database schema. You might have a separate table for roles and another for permissions, with relationships to the users table.

3. Best Practices

HTTPS: Use HTTPS to encrypt communication between the client and server, protecting session data from interception.

HttpOnly Cookies: Set the `HttpOnly` flag for session cookies to prevent them from being accessed by JavaScript, mitigating the risk of cross-site scripting (XSS) attacks.

Secure Cookies: Use the `Secure` flag for cookies to ensure they are only transmitted over HTTPS connections.

Session Fixation: Prevent session fixation attacks by regenerating session IDs after login.

Principle of Least Privilege: Grant users only the necessary permissions to perform their tasks.

4. Code Example (PHP with Session)

PHP

```php
// Check if the user is logged in and has admin
role

session_start();



if          (isset($_SESSION['user_id'])          &&
$_SESSION['role'] === 'admin') {

  // Allow access to admin panel

} else {

  // Redirect to login page

  header('Location: login.php');

  exit;

}
```

By effectively managing user sessions and implementing robust permission systems, you can enhance the security and usability of your web application. Remember to prioritize security considerations and follow best practices to protect user data and prevent unauthorized access.

Chapter 7

Working with Forms and User Input

7.1 Handling and Validating User Data

User input is the lifeblood of many web applications, but it can also be a source of errors and security vulnerabilities if not handled correctly. This chapter explores the crucial process of handling and validating user data to ensure data integrity, prevent malicious attacks, and provide a smooth user experience.

1. Why Validate?

Data Integrity: Validation ensures that data conforms to the expected format and rules, preventing inconsistencies and errors in your database.

Security: Validation helps prevent malicious input that could lead to security vulnerabilities like SQL injection, cross-site scripting (XSS), and command injection.

User Experience: Clear and informative validation feedback guides users in providing correct information, leading to a smoother and more efficient user experience.

2. Types of Validation

Data Type Validation: Verify that the input matches the expected data type (e.g., integer, string, email, date).

Range Checks: Ensure that numeric input falls within a specific range.

Format Validation: Check that data adheres to a specific format (e.g., phone number, postal code).

Presence Validation: Ensure that required fields are not empty.

Uniqueness Validation: Verify that data is unique within a specific context (e.g., username, email address).

Custom Validation: Implement custom validation rules based on your application's specific requirements.

3. Validation Techniques

Client-Side Validation: Use JavaScript to perform validation in the user's browser. This provides immediate feedback and improves user experience.

Server-Side Validation: Perform validation on the server using PHP or your chosen back-end language. This is essential for security and data integrity, as client-side validation can be bypassed.

Database Constraints: Utilize database constraints (e.g., `NOT NULL`, `UNIQUE`, `CHECK`) to enforce data integrity at the database level.

4. Error Handling and Feedback

Clear Error Messages: Provide informative and user-friendly error messages that clearly explain the validation issue and guide the user in correcting it.

Inline Validation: Display error messages next to the input fields for immediate feedback.

Error Summaries: Provide a summary of all validation errors at the top of the form for a comprehensive overview.

5. Security Considerations

Sanitize Input: Sanitize user input to remove or escape potentially harmful characters that could be used for attacks like XSS.

Prevent SQL Injection: Use parameterized queries or prepared statements to prevent SQL injection vulnerabilities.

Protect Against Cross-Site Request Forgery (CSRF): Implement CSRF tokens to prevent unauthorized form submissions.

6. Code Example (PHP)

PHP

```php
// Validate an email address

if                         (filter_var($email,
FILTER_VALIDATE_EMAIL)) {

  // Email is valid

} else {

  // Email is invalid

    $errorMessage  =  "Please  enter  a  valid
email address.";

}



// Validate a numeric input
```

```php
if (is_numeric($age) && $age >= 18 && $age
<= 120) {

  // Age is valid

} else {

  // Age is invalid

  $errorMessage = "Please enter a valid age
between 18 and 120.";

}
```

By implementing thorough data validation and handling user input with care, you can enhance the security, reliability, and user-friendliness of your web application. Remember that validation is a crucial step in ensuring data integrity and protecting against potential threats.

7.2 File Uploads and Security Considerations

Allowing users to upload files adds valuable functionality to web applications, but it also introduces potential security risks if not handled carefully. This chapter outlines how to implement file uploads securely, protecting your application and users from malicious attacks.

1. Handling File Uploads

HTML Form: Use an HTML form with `enctype="multipart/form-data"` to allow users to select and upload files.

HTML

```html
<form action="upload.php" method="post"
enctype="multipart/form-data">

  Select file to upload:

    <input type="file" name="fileToUpload"
id="fileToUpload">

    <input type="submit" value="Upload¹ File"
name="submit">²

</form>
```

Server-Side Processing: Use server-side code (e.g., PHP) to process the uploaded file. Access file information using the `$_FILES` superglobal in PHP.

PHP

```php
if(isset($_POST["submit"])) {

  $target_dir = "uploads/";

    $target_file = $target_dir .
basename($_FILES["fileToUpload"]["name"]);

    // ... perform validation and security
checks ...
```

```php
                                                 if
(move_uploaded_file($_FILES["fileToUpload"][
"tmp_name"], $target_file)) {

    // File uploaded successfully

  } else {

    // File upload failed

  }

}
```

2. Security Considerations

File Type Validation: Restrict the allowed file types to prevent uploads of potentially dangerous files (e.g., executable scripts, malware). Validate file extensions and MIME types.

PHP

```php
$allowed_types = array("jpg", "jpeg", "png",
"gif");

$file_extension                              =
strtolower(pathinfo($target_file,PATHINFO_EX
TENSION));

if(!in_array($file_extension,
$allowed_types))³ {
```

```
    // Invalid file type

}
```

File Size Limits: Set limits on the maximum allowed file size to prevent denial-of-service (DoS) attacks and excessive storage usage.

PHP

```
if      ($_FILES["fileToUpload"]["size"]      >
500000) { // 500KB limit

    // File size too large

}
```

Filename Sanitization: Sanitize filenames to remove potentially harmful characters and prevent directory traversal attacks.

PHP

```
$target_file      =      $target_dir      .
basename(preg_replace("/[^a-zA-Z0-9.\-\_]/",
"", $_FILES["fileToUpload"]["name"]));
```

File Content Scanning: Scan uploaded files for malware and other malicious content using antivirus software or dedicated file scanning tools.

Storage Location: Store uploaded files outside the web root directory to prevent direct access via URLs.

Access Control: Implement access control mechanisms to restrict who can upload, access, and download files.

User Authentication: Require user authentication before allowing file uploads to track who uploaded which files.

3. Additional Security Measures

Rename Uploaded Files: Rename uploaded files to avoid filename collisions and potential vulnerabilities related to original filenames.

Use a Content Delivery Network (CDN): Store files on a CDN to improve performance and security.

Implement Rate Limiting: Limit the number of file uploads per user or IP address within a given timeframe to prevent abuse.

Monitor File Upload Activity: Monitor file upload logs to detect suspicious activity and potential attacks.

4. Code Example (PHP with File Upload and Validation)

PHP

```php
if(isset($_POST["submit"])) {

    $target_dir = "uploads/";
```

```php
$target_file       =     $target_dir    .
basename($_FILES["fileToUpload"]["name"]);

$uploadOk = 1;

$imageFileType          =
strtolower(pathinfo($target_file,PATHINFO_EX
TENSION));[4]


// Check if image file is a actual image
or fake image

if(isset($_POST["submit"])) {

$check      =
getimagesize($_FILES["fileToUpload"]["tmp_na
me"]);

if($check !== false)[5] {

// File is an image

$uploadOk = 1;

} else {

// File is not an image

$uploadOk = 0;

}
```

```php
}


// Check if file already exists

if (file_exists($target_file))[6] {

  // File already exists

  $uploadOk = 0;

}



// Check file size

    if  ($_FILES["fileToUpload"]["size"]  >
500000) {

  // File size too large

  $uploadOk = 0;

}



// Allow certain file formats
```

```php
        if($imageFileType    !=    "jpg"    &&
$imageFileType != "png" && $imageFileType !=
"jpeg"

   && $imageFileType != "gif" ) {

    // Invalid file type

    $uploadOk = 0;

  }




    // Check if $uploadOk7 is set to 0 by an
error

  if ($uploadOk == 0) {

    // File upload failed

  } else {

                                        if
(move_uploaded_file($_FILES["fileToUpload"][
"tmp_name"], $target_file)) {

      // File uploaded successfully

    } else {

      // File upload failed

    }
```

```
    }

  }
```

By implementing these security measures and best practices, you can ensure that file uploads are handled safely and responsibly, protecting your application and users from potential threats.

7.3 Building Dynamic Forms with JavaScript

Static forms can be limiting when it comes to providing a user-friendly and interactive experience. JavaScript empowers you to create dynamic forms that adapt to user input, provide real-time validation, and enhance the overall user experience. This chapter explores the techniques and concepts involved in building dynamic forms with JavaScript.

1. Adding and Removing Form Fields

JavaScript allows you to dynamically add or remove form fields based on user interactions or specific conditions. This is particularly useful for forms with variable numbers of inputs, such as adding multiple items to a shopping cart or creating a survey with optional questions.

JavaScript

```
// Add a new input field

const          newInput          =
document.createElement('input');

newInput.type = 'text';
```

```javascript
newInput.name = 'item[]';

document.getElementById('form-container').ap
pendChild(newInput);



// Remove an input field

const            inputToRemove            =
document.getElementById('specific-input');

inputToRemove.remove();
```

2. Showing and Hiding Form Fields

You can dynamically show or hide form fields based on user selections or other conditions. This can simplify forms and prevent users from being overwhelmed with unnecessary inputs.

JavaScript

```javascript
// Show a hidden field

document.getElementById('hidden-field').styl
e.display = 'block';



// Hide a visible field

document.getElementById('visible-field').sty
le.display = 'none';
```

3. Real-time Validation

JavaScript enables real-time validation, providing immediate feedback to users as they fill out the form. This prevents errors and improves the user experience.

JavaScript

```
// Validate an email field in real-time

const               emailInput              =
document.getElementById('email');

emailInput.addEventListener('input',
function() {

  if (validateEmail(emailInput.value))[1] {

    // Display a success message

  } else {

    // Display an error message

  }

});
```

4. Dynamic Form Submission

JavaScript can handle form submissions asynchronously using AJAX, preventing page reloads and providing a smoother user experience.

JavaScript

```
// Submit form data using AJAX

const                    form                    =
document.getElementById('myForm');

form.addEventListener('submit',
function(event) {

  event.preventDefault(); // Prevent default
form submission[2]



  // Gather form data

  // ...



  // Send data to server using AJAX

  // ...

});
```

5. Advanced Form Features

Auto-completion: Suggest options to users as they type in input fields, improving efficiency and user experience.

Conditional Logic: Dynamically adjust form fields or sections based on user selections or input values.

Form Wizards: Break down long forms into multiple steps, guiding users through the process and improving completion rates.

Drag-and-Drop Functionality: Allow users to drag and drop elements within a form to rearrange or customize the layout.

6. Libraries and Frameworks

JavaScript libraries and frameworks like jQuery, React, Angular, and Vue.js provide tools and components that simplify the development of dynamic forms. They offer features like data binding, form validation, and state management, making it easier to create complex and interactive forms.

7. Example: Adding Dynamic Fields

HTML

```html
<!DOCTYPE html>

<html>

<head>

  <title>Dynamic Form</title>

</head>

<body>
```

```
<form id="myForm">

    <div id="form-container">

        <input type="text" name="item[]">

    </div>

                        <button      type="button"
onclick="addInput()">Add Input</button>

    <button type="submit">Submit</button>

</form>


<script>

    function addInput() {

                    const      newInput     =
document.createElement('input');

        newInput.type = 'text';

        newInput.name = 'item[]';


document.getElementById('form-container').ap
pendChild(newInput);

    }
```

```
</script>

</body>

</html>
```

By mastering these techniques and leveraging the power of JavaScript, you can create dynamic forms that enhance user interaction, improve data integrity, and provide a more engaging and efficient user experience.

Chapter 8

RESTful APIs and AJAX

8.1 Building APIs with PHP and JSON

APIs (Application Programming Interfaces) are the backbone of modern web applications, allowing different systems to communicate and exchange data. This chapter focuses on building APIs with PHP and JSON (JavaScript Object Notation), a popular data format for web services.

1. RESTful API Principles

REST (Representational State Transfer) is an architectural style for designing networked applications. RESTful APIs adhere[1] to these principles:

Client-Server Architecture: Separation of concerns between the client (front-end) and server (back-end).

Statelessness: Each request from the client to the server must contain all the information necessary to understand the request.[2]

Cacheability: Responses from the server should explicitly state whether they can be cached or not.

Uniform Interface: Use standard HTTP methods (GET, POST, PUT, DELETE) for consistent interaction with resources.

Layered System: The client cannot ordinarily tell whether it is connected directly to the end server or an intermediary along the way.

Code on Demand (optional):[3] Servers can temporarily extend or customize the functionality of a client by transferring executable code.[4]

2. Defining API Endpoints

API endpoints are URLs that represent specific resources or actions. For example:

`/api/users`: Retrieve a list of users.

`/api/users/1`: Retrieve a specific user with ID 1.

`/api/products`: Retrieve a list of products.

3. Handling API Requests

Use PHP to handle API requests, process data, and interact with the database.

PHP

```php
// Example using a PHP framework like
Laravel

Route::get('/api/users', function () {

  $users = User::all();

  return response()->json($users);

});


Route::post('/api/users', function (Request $request) {

  $user = new User;
```

```php
$user->name = $request->input('name');

$user->email = $request->input('email');

$user->save();

    return response()->json($user,⁵ 201); // 201 Created

});
```

4. JSON for Data Exchange

JSON is a lightweight data format that is easy to read and parse by both humans and machines. Use PHP's `json_encode()` function to convert data into JSON format for API responses.

PHP

```php
$data = ['name' => 'Alice', 'email' => 'alice@example.com'];

$jsonResponse = json_encode($data);
```

5. HTTP Status Codes

Use appropriate HTTP status codes to indicate the success or failure of API requests.

200 OK: Successful request.

201 Created: Resource created successfully.

400 Bad Request: The request was malformed or invalid.

401 Unauthorized: Authentication required.

404 Not Found: Resource not found.

500 Internal Server Error: Server error.

6. API Documentation

Provide clear and comprehensive API documentation to help developers understand how to use your API. Tools like Swagger or Postman can be used to generate API documentation.

7. Security Considerations

Authentication: Implement authentication mechanisms (e.g., API keys, OAuth) to secure your API.

Authorization: Control access to API resources based on user roles and permissions.

Input Validation: Validate and sanitize all input data to prevent vulnerabilities.

Rate Limiting: Limit the number of requests from a particular IP address to prevent abuse.

8. Example: Simple API Endpoint with PHP

PHP

```php
<?php

header('Content-Type: application/json');



// Database connection (replace with your
credentials)
```

```php
$servername = "localhost";

$username = "username";

$password = "password";

$dbname = "myDB";


try {

    $conn = new PDO("mysql:host=$servername;dbname=$dbname", $username, $password);

    $conn->setAttribute(PDO::ATTR_ERRMODE,[6] PDO::ERRMODE_EXCEPTION);[7]


    // Get the ID from the request

    $id = $_GET['id'];


    // Prepare and execute the SQL query

    $stmt = $conn->prepare("SELECT * FROM users WHERE id = :id");

    $stmt->bindParam(':id', $id);
```

```php
    $stmt->execute();


    // Fetch the result

    $user = $stmt->fetch(PDO::FETCH_ASSOC);



    // Return the user data as JSON

    echo json_encode($user);



} catch(PDOException $e) {

    echo json_encode(['error' => 'Database
error: ' . $e->getMessage()]);

}

$conn = null;

?>
```

By following these guidelines and best practices, you can build robust and secure APIs with PHP and JSON, enabling seamless communication and data exchange between different systems.

8.2 Asynchronous JavaScript and XML (AJAX) for Dynamic Content

AJAX (Asynchronous JavaScript and XML) revolutionized web development by enabling dynamic content updates without requiring full page reloads. This chapter delves into the core concepts and techniques of AJAX, empowering you to create more responsive and interactive web experiences.

1. The Power of Asynchronicity

Traditional web pages require a full reload to update content, leading to a disruptive user experience. AJAX allows you to send and receive data from the server in the background, updating only specific parts of the page without interrupting the user's flow.

2. The XMLHttpRequest Object

The `XMLHttpRequest` object is the heart of AJAX. It allows you to make HTTP requests to the server from JavaScript.

JavaScript

```
const xhr = new XMLHttpRequest();

xhr.open('GET', 'data.json'); // Set request
method and URL

xhr.send(); // Send the request
```

3. Handling Responses

Use event handlers to process the server's response.

JavaScript

```javascript
xhr.onload = function() {

    if (xhr.status === 200) { // Check for
successful response

                    const        data        =
JSON.parse(xhr.responseText); // Parse JSON
response

        // Update the page with the received
data

    } else {

    // Handle errors

    }

};
```

4. Updating the Page

Use JavaScript's DOM manipulation capabilities to update the page with the received data.

JavaScript

```javascript
// Example: Update a div with new content

document.getElementById('myDiv').innerHTML =
data.content;
```

5. Modern AJAX with Fetch API

The Fetch API provides a more modern and streamlined approach to making AJAX requests.

JavaScript

```javascript
fetch('data.json')

  .then(response => response.json())

  .then(data => {

    // Process the fetched data

  })

  .catch(error => {

    // Handle errors

  });
```

6. Use Cases for AJAX

Form Submissions: Submit forms without page reloads, providing immediate feedback to users.

Dynamic Content Loading: Load content on demand, such as comments, product details, or search results.

Real-time Updates: Display real-time updates, such as notifications, chat messages, or stock prices.

Autocompletion: Suggest options to users as they type, enhancing form interactions.

7. Security Considerations

Same-Origin Policy: AJAX requests are subject to the same-origin policy, which restricts requests to the same domain, protocol, and port.

Cross-Origin Resource Sharing (CORS): If you need to make requests to a different domain, configure CORS on the server to allow cross-origin requests.

Input Validation: Validate and sanitize all data received from the server to prevent XSS attacks.

8. Example: Loading Content with AJAX

JavaScript

```javascript
function loadContent() {

    const xhr = new XMLHttpRequest();

    xhr.open('GET', 'content.html');

    xhr.onload = function() {

        if (xhr.status === 200) {


document.getElementById('content-container')
.innerHTML = xhr.responseText;

        }

    };
```

```
      xhr.send();


   }
```

By mastering AJAX, you can create dynamic and responsive web applications that provide a seamless user experience. Asynchronous data fetching and partial page updates enhance interactivity and engagement, making your web applications more user-friendly and efficient.

8.3 Consuming APIs from Web Applications

Web applications often rely on external APIs to access data and services, enriching their functionality and user experience. This chapter focuses on consuming APIs from your web application, covering techniques for making API requests, handling responses, and integrating data into your front-end.

1. Identifying API Endpoints

Before consuming an API, you need to identify the relevant endpoints that provide the data or services you require. API documentation is crucial for understanding the available endpoints, request parameters, and response formats.

2. Making API Requests

Use JavaScript's `fetch` API or `XMLHttpRequest` object to make HTTP requests to the API endpoints.

JavaScript

```
   // Using Fetch API
```

```javascript
fetch('https://api.example.com/users')

  .then(response => response.json())

  .then(data => {

    // Process the fetched data

  });



// Using XMLHttpRequest

const xhr = new XMLHttpRequest();

xhr.open('GET',
'https://api.example.com/products');

xhr.onload = function() {

  if (xhr.status === 200) {

                 const       data       =
JSON.parse(xhr.responseText);

    // Process the data

  }

};

xhr.send();
```

3. Handling API Responses

API responses typically come in JSON or XML format. Parse the response data using JavaScript's `JSON.parse()` or XML parsing techniques.

4. Displaying Data in the Front-End

Use JavaScript's DOM manipulation capabilities to display the fetched data in your web application.

JavaScript

```
// Example: Displaying a list of users

const              userList              =
document.getElementById('user-list');

data.forEach(user => {

        const         listItem         =
document.createElement('li');

  listItem.textContent = user.name;[1]

  userList.appendChild(listItem);[2]

});
```

5. Authentication and Authorization

If the API requires authentication, include the necessary credentials (e.g., API keys, access tokens) in your requests.

JavaScript

```javascript
// Example with API key in headers

fetch('https://api.example.com/data', {

  headers: {

    'Authorization': 'Bearer your_api_key'

  }

})

  .then(response => response.json())

  // ...
```

6. Error Handling

Implement error handling to gracefully handle API errors and provide informative feedback to users.

JavaScript

```javascript
fetch('https://api.example.com/data')

  .then(response => {
```

```
    if (!response.ok) {

        throw new Error('Network response was
not ok');

    }

    return response.json();

})

.then(data³ => {

    // Process the⁴ data

})

.catch(error => {

    console.error('There has been a problem
with your fetch operation:', error);

    // Display an error message to the user

});
```

7. Cross-Origin Resource Sharing (CORS)

If your web application is making requests to an API on a different
domain, ensure that CORS is properly configured on the API
server to allow cross-origin requests.

8. API Rate Limiting

Be mindful of API rate limits and implement strategies to handle rate limiting errors, such as retrying requests after a delay or displaying appropriate messages to users.

9. Example: Displaying Weather Data

JavaScript

```javascript
// Fetch weather data from OpenWeatherMap
API

fetch(`https://api.openweathermap.org/data/2
.5/weather?q=London&appid=your_api_key`)

  .then(response => response.json())

  .then(data => {

document.getElementById('city').textContent
= data.name;

document.getElementById('temperature').textC
ontent = data.main.temp;[5]

  });
```

By understanding these techniques and best practices, you can effectively consume APIs from your web applications, enriching their functionality and providing valuable services to your users.

Remember to always refer to the API documentation and prioritize security considerations when interacting with external APIs.

Chapter 9

Performance Optimization and Security

9.1 Caching Techniques for Faster Loading Times

In the fast-paced world of the web, speed is paramount. Users expect websites to load quickly, and caching plays a crucial role in achieving optimal performance. This chapter explores various caching techniques that can significantly reduce loading times and enhance the user experience.

1. Browser Caching

Leverage the user's browser to store static assets (images, CSS, JavaScript files) locally. This allows returning visitors to load these assets from their cache instead of downloading them again, resulting in faster page loads.

Cache-Control Headers: Use HTTP headers like `Cache-Control`, `Expires`, and `ETag` to instruct browsers how long to cache specific resources.

.htaccess: For Apache servers, utilize `.htaccess` files to set cache-control headers for different file types.

2. Content Delivery Network (CDN)

CDNs store copies of your website's assets on servers distributed geographically. When a user requests your website, the CDN serves the assets from the server closest to their location, reducing latency and improving loading times.

3. Server-Side Caching

Implement caching mechanisms on your server to store frequently accessed data or rendered pages.

Object Caching: Cache the results of expensive operations, such as database queries or API calls, to avoid redundant computations.

Page Caching: Cache entire HTML pages to serve them directly from the cache, bypassing server-side processing.

Opcode Caching: Cache compiled PHP code (opcodes) to reduce the overhead of parsing and compiling code on each request. Popular opcode caching tools include OPcache and APC.

4. Database Caching

Optimize database performance by caching frequently accessed data or query results.

Query Caching: Cache the results of frequently executed database queries to avoid redundant database access.

Object-Relational Mapping (ORM) Caching: Utilize ORM frameworks like Eloquent (Laravel) or Doctrine (Symfony) to cache database objects and relationships.

5. Caching Dynamic Content

Caching dynamic content can be more challenging, but techniques like fragment caching and reverse proxy caching can be effective.

Fragment Caching: Cache specific parts of a dynamically generated page, such as a sidebar or a list of recent posts.

Reverse Proxy Caching: Use a reverse proxy server (e.g., Varnish) to cache dynamic content based on various criteria, such as URL, headers, or cookies.

6. Cache Invalidation

Implement mechanisms to invalidate cached content when it becomes outdated. This ensures that users always see the latest version of your website.

7. Monitoring and Optimization

Regularly monitor your caching strategy to identify areas for improvement. Analyze cache hit rates, loading times, and server resource usage to optimize your caching configuration.

8. Tools and Technologies

Redis: A high-performance in-memory data store that can be used for caching.

Memcached: Another popular in-memory caching system.

Caching Libraries: Utilize caching libraries provided by your framework or language to simplify caching implementation.

By implementing a comprehensive caching strategy and utilizing the appropriate tools and techniques, you can significantly improve the performance of your web application. Faster loading times enhance user experience, reduce server load, and contribute to a more efficient and enjoyable web browsing experience.

9.2 Database Optimization and Query Tuning

A well-optimized database is crucial for the performance and scalability of your web application. This chapter explores techniques for database optimization and query tuning, ensuring efficient data retrieval and overall application responsiveness.

1. Database Design

Normalization: Properly normalize your database schema to minimize redundancy and improve data integrity.

Data Types: Choose appropriate data types for each column to optimize storage and query performance.

Relationships: Define clear relationships between tables using primary and foreign keys.

2. Indexing

Identify Frequently Accessed Columns: Create indexes on columns frequently used in `WHERE` clauses, `JOIN` conditions, and `ORDER BY` clauses.

Types of Indexes: Utilize different types of indexes (e.g., single-column, composite, unique) based on your query patterns.

Avoid Over-Indexing: Too many indexes can slow down write operations.

3. Query Optimization

Analyze Query Performance: Use tools like `EXPLAIN` (MySQL) to analyze query execution plans and identify bottlenecks.

Optimize `WHERE` Clauses: Use efficient filtering conditions and avoid unnecessary wildcards.

Optimize `JOIN` Operations: Use appropriate join types and ensure proper indexing on joined columns.

Limit Data Retrieval: Retrieve only the necessary data using `SELECT` specific columns and `LIMIT` clauses.

Avoid `SELECT *`: Specify the columns you need instead of retrieving all columns.

4. Database Configuration

Memory Allocation: Allocate sufficient memory to the database server to improve caching and query performance.

Query Cache: Enable and configure the query cache to store results of frequently executed queries.

Buffer Pool: Adjust the buffer pool size to optimize data caching in memory.

5. Hardware Considerations

Disk I/O: Use fast storage devices (e.g., SSDs) to improve disk read/write performance.

CPU and Memory: Ensure your server has sufficient CPU and memory resources to handle database operations.

6. Query Tuning Tools

Database Profilers: Use profiling tools to identify slow queries and analyze their execution time.

Query Optimizers: Utilize query optimization tools to suggest improvements to your SQL queries.

7. Code Examples (MySQL)

Using `EXPLAIN`:

SQL

```
EXPLAIN SELECT * FROM users WHERE username =
'john_doe';
```

Optimizing a `JOIN` **query:**

SQL

```
-- Inefficient

SELECT *

 FROM orders o, customers c

WHERE o.customer_id = c.id;



-- Efficient

SELECT o.*, c.name

FROM orders o

INNER JOIN customers c ON o.customer_id =
c.id;
```

8. Regular Monitoring and Maintenance

Monitor Database Performance: Regularly monitor database performance metrics (e.g., query execution time, resource usage) to identify potential issues.

Optimize Table Statistics: Update table statistics periodically to ensure the query optimizer has accurate information.

Defragment Tables: Defragment tables to reduce disk fragmentation and improve data access.

By implementing these database optimization and query tuning techniques, you can significantly enhance the performance and scalability of your web application. Regularly monitor and maintain your database to ensure optimal performance and adapt to evolving data and usage patterns.

9.3 Protecting Against Common Web Vulnerabilities

Web applications are constantly under threat from a variety of vulnerabilities that can compromise sensitive data, disrupt services, and damage reputation. This chapter outlines common web vulnerabilities and provides strategies to protect your applications.

1. Cross-Site Scripting (XSS)

XSS allows attackers to inject malicious scripts into web pages viewed by other users. These scripts can steal cookies, hijack sessions, or redirect users to malicious sites.

Prevention:

Input Sanitization: Sanitize all user input to escape special characters (e.g., $<$, $>$, ") that could be interpreted as HTML or JavaScript code.

Output Encoding: Encode data dynamically displayed on the page to prevent malicious scripts from being executed.

Content Security Policy (CSP): Implement CSP headers to restrict the sources from which scripts can be loaded, limiting the impact of XSS attacks.

2. SQL Injection

SQL injection occurs when attackers insert malicious SQL code into user input, manipulating database queries to gain unauthorized access or modify data.

Prevention:

Prepared Statements: Use prepared statements with parameterized queries to separate SQL code from user input.

Input Validation: Validate and sanitize all user input to prevent malicious SQL code from being executed.

Database Access Controls: Limit database user privileges to the minimum necessary for the application.

3. Cross-Site Request Forgery (CSRF)

CSRF tricks users into performing unwanted actions on a web application while they are authenticated. This can lead to unauthorized data modification or fund transfers.

Prevention:

CSRF Tokens: Generate unique tokens for each user session and include them in forms to verify that the request originated from the legitimate user.

SameSite Cookies: Use the `SameSite` attribute for cookies to restrict their transmission to requests originating from the same site.

Double Submit Cookies: Include a hidden field with a copy of the CSRF token in the form, and verify that both the cookie and the hidden field contain the same value.

4. Authentication and Authorization Vulnerabilities

Weaknesses in authentication and authorization mechanisms can allow attackers to gain unauthorized access to accounts or sensitive data.

Prevention:

Strong Passwords: Enforce strong password policies and encourage users to use unique passwords.

Multi-Factor Authentication (MFA): Implement MFA to add an extra layer of security.

Secure Session Management: Use secure session management practices, including session timeouts, regeneration, and HTTPS.

Role-Based Access Control (RBAC): Implement RBAC to control access to resources based on user roles.

5. Security Misconfiguration

Misconfigured servers, frameworks, or applications can expose vulnerabilities that attackers can exploit.

Prevention:

Regular Updates: Keep software and frameworks updated to patch known vulnerabilities.

Secure Configuration: Follow security best practices for configuring servers, frameworks, and applications.

Disable Unnecessary Features: Disable any unnecessary features or services to reduce the attack surface.

6. Sensitive Data Exposure

Failing to protect sensitive data (e.g., credit card information, personal data) can lead to data breaches and privacy violations.

Prevention:

Data Encryption: Encrypt sensitive data both in transit (using HTTPS) and at rest (using database encryption).

Access Controls: Restrict access to sensitive data to authorized personnel only.

Data Minimization: Collect and store only the necessary data.

7. Using Components with Known Vulnerabilities

Using outdated or vulnerable third-party components (libraries, frameworks) can introduce security risks.

Prevention:

Regular Dependency Checks: Regularly check for updates and vulnerabilities in your project's dependencies.

Vulnerability Scanning: Use vulnerability scanning tools to identify potential weaknesses in your application.

Use Reputable Components: Choose well-maintained and reputable components from trusted sources.

8. Insufficient Logging and Monitoring

Lack of proper logging and monitoring can hinder the detection and response to security incidents.

Prevention:

Enable Logging: Enable detailed logging of application events and security-related activities.

Monitor Logs: Regularly monitor logs for suspicious activity.

Intrusion Detection Systems (IDS): Consider using IDS to detect and alert on potential attacks.

By understanding these common web vulnerabilities and implementing appropriate preventive measures, you can significantly strengthen the security of your web applications and protect user data. Remember that security is an ongoing process that requires continuous vigilance and adaptation to evolving threats.

Chapter 10

Deployment and Beyond

10.1 Deploying Your Application to a Web Server

Deploying your web application is the exciting culmination of your hard work, making it accessible to users around the world. This chapter guides you through the process of deploying your PHP and MySQL application to a web server, covering essential steps and considerations.

1. Choosing a Web Hosting Provider

Select a web hosting provider that meets your application's needs and budget. Consider factors like:

Shared Hosting: Affordable option suitable for small applications with low traffic.

Virtual Private Server (VPS): Offers more control and resources than shared hosting, ideal for growing applications.

Cloud Hosting: Provides scalability and flexibility, allowing you to adjust resources as needed.

Dedicated Server: Offers the highest level of control and performance, suitable for high-traffic applications.

2. Preparing Your Application

Before deployment, ensure your application is ready for production:

Optimize Code: Minify CSS and JavaScript files, optimize images, and implement caching techniques to improve performance.

Database Configuration: Update database credentials in your application's configuration files to match the production database.

Error Handling: Implement robust error handling and logging to identify and address issues in the production environment.

Security: Review and strengthen security measures, including input validation, authentication, and authorization.

3. Transferring Files

Transfer your application files to the web server using secure methods like:

Secure File Transfer Protocol (SFTP): A secure file transfer protocol that encrypts data during transfer.

File Transfer Protocol Secure (FTPS): An extension of FTP that adds SSL/TLS encryption for secure transfer.

Git: Use Git to deploy your application from a repository, ensuring version control and easy rollback.

4. Setting Up the Web Server

Configure the web server to host your application:

Apache or Nginx: Install and configure Apache or Nginx as the web server.

PHP: Install and configure PHP to process your application's code.

MySQL: Install and configure MySQL as the database server.

Virtual Hosts: Configure virtual hosts to map your domain name to your application's directory.

.htaccess: Configure `.htaccess` files (for Apache) to handle URL rewriting, redirects, and other server-side configurations.

5. Database Migration

Migrate your database schema and data to the production database:

Export/Import: Export your database from your development environment and import it into the production database.

Migration Scripts: Use migration scripts to create and update the database schema in the production environment.

6. Testing and Deployment

Thoroughly test your application in the production environment to ensure everything works as expected.

Functional Testing: Test all features and functionalities to ensure they work correctly.

Performance Testing: Test the application's performance under expected load to identify potential bottlenecks.

Security Testing: Perform security testing to identify and address any vulnerabilities.

Once testing is complete, make your application live by pointing your domain name to the web server.

7. Post-Deployment Monitoring

Monitor your application after deployment to identify and address any issues that may arise.

Error Logs: Regularly check error logs for any errors or exceptions.

Performance Monitoring: Monitor server resource usage and application performance to ensure optimal performance.

Security Monitoring: Monitor security logs and implement intrusion detection systems to identify and respond to potential attacks.

8. Deployment Tools

Utilize deployment tools to automate and streamline the deployment process.

Git: Use Git for version control and automated deployments.

Deployment Scripts: Create scripts to automate tasks like file transfer, database migration, and server configuration.

Continuous Integration/Continuous Deployment (CI/CD): Implement CI/CD pipelines to automate the build, testing, and deployment[1] process.

By following these steps and best practices, you can successfully deploy your PHP and MySQL application to a web server, making it accessible to users and realizing the fruits of your development efforts. Remember to prioritize security, performance, and ongoing monitoring to ensure a smooth and successful deployment.

10.2 Version Control with Git

Version control is an essential practice for any software development project, and Git has emerged as the leading version control system. This chapter introduces you to Git, exploring its core concepts and how it can streamline your development workflow.

1. What is Git?

Git is a distributed version control system that tracks changes to files over time. It allows you to:

Record Changes: Keep a detailed history of every modification made to your project files.

Revert to Previous Versions: Easily revert to earlier versions of your code if needed.

Branch and Merge: Create separate branches for new features or bug fixes, and merge them back into the main codebase when ready.

Collaborate: Work effectively with other developers on the same project.

2. Basic Git Workflow

Initialize a Repository: Create a new Git repository using `git init`.

Stage Changes: Stage changes to be committed using `git add`.

Commit Changes: Commit staged changes with a descriptive message using `git commit -m "Your message"`.

Push Changes: Push your local commits to a remote repository (e.g., GitHub, GitLab) using `git push`.

Pull Changes: Pull the latest changes from a remote repository to your local machine using `git pull`.

3. Branching and Merging

Create a Branch: Create a new branch for a specific feature or bug fix using `git checkout -b branch-name`.

Switch Branches: Switch between different branches using `git checkout branch-name`.

Merge Branches: Merge changes from one branch into another using `git merge branch-name`.

4. Remote Repositories

Clone a Repository: Clone a remote repository to your local machine using `git clone repository-url`.

Add a Remote: Add a remote repository to your local project using `git remote add origin repository-url`.

Push and Pull: Push your local commits to the remote repository and pull changes from the remote to your local machine.

5. Common Git Commands

`git status`: View the status of your working directory and staging area.

`git log`: View the commit history of your project.

`git diff`: See the differences between your working directory and the last commit.

`git reset`: Undo changes or unstage files.

`git checkout`: Switch branches or restore files to a previous version.

6. Collaboration with Git

Forking: Create a copy of a remote repository on your own account.

Pull Requests: Propose changes to a repository by submitting a pull request.

Code Reviews: Review code changes proposed by other developers.

7. Git Hosting Services

GitHub: A popular platform for hosting Git repositories and collaborating on projects.

GitLab: Another popular Git hosting service with features like CI/CD pipelines.

Bitbucket: A Git hosting service often used for private repositories.

8. Benefits of Using Git

Version Control: Track changes, revert to previous versions, and manage code history effectively.

Collaboration: Facilitate collaboration among developers.

Branching and Merging: Enable parallel development and feature isolation.

Code Reusability: Promote code reuse and modular development.

Backup and Recovery: Provide a backup of your codebase and facilitate easy recovery.

9. Example: Basic Git Workflow

Bash

```bash
# Initialize a Git repository

git init


# Stage changes

git add .
```

```
# Commit changes

git commit -m "Initial commit"


# Add a remote repository

git          remote          add          origin
https://github.com/your-username/your-reposi
tory.git


# Push changes to the remote repository

git push -u origin main
```

By mastering Git, you gain a powerful tool for managing your codebase, collaborating with others, and ensuring the integrity of your project. Its distributed nature, branching capabilities, and extensive ecosystem make it an indispensable tool for modern software development.

10.3 Continuous Integration and Continuous Deployment (CI/CD)

Continuous Integration and Continuous Deployment (CI/CD) are cornerstones of modern software development, enabling teams to deliver high-quality software rapidly and reliably.[1] This chapter explores the concepts and benefits of CI/CD and how to implement it in your PHP and MySQL projects.

1. Continuous Integration (CI)

CI is a practice where developers integrate code changes into a shared repository frequently, ideally several times a day.[2] Each integration triggers an automated build and test process, ensuring that the new code doesn't introduce errors or break existing functionality.[3]

Benefits of CI:

Early Bug Detection: Identify and address bugs early in the development cycle.[4]

Improved Code Quality: Ensure code consistency and adherence to coding standards.[5]

Reduced Integration Risks: Minimize the risks associated with merging code from multiple developers.[6]

Faster Feedback Loops: Provide rapid feedback to developers on the quality and impact of their code changes.[7]

2. Continuous Deployment (CD)

CD extends CI by automating the release and deployment of code changes to production environments.[8] This means that every change that passes the automated tests is automatically deployed to users.[9]

Benefits of CD:

Faster Time to Market: Deliver new features and updates to users more quickly.[10]

Reduced Deployment Risks: Minimize manual errors and inconsistencies in the deployment process.[11]

Increased Efficiency: Free up developers from manual deployment tasks, allowing them to focus on development.[12]

Improved Collaboration: Promote collaboration between development and operations teams.[13]

3. The CI/CD Pipeline

A CI/CD pipeline is a series of automated steps that code changes go through from development to production.[14] Typical stages include:

Build: Compile code, run unit tests, and package the application.[15]

Test: Execute various tests, such as integration tests, end-to-end tests, and performance tests.[16]

Deploy: Deploy the application to staging or production environments.[17]

Monitor: Monitor the application in production for errors and performance issues.

4. Implementing CI/CD

Version Control: Use a version control system like Git to manage code changes and trigger the CI/CD pipeline.[18]

CI/CD Tools: Utilize CI/CD tools like Jenkins, GitLab CI/CD, GitHub Actions, or CircleCI to automate the pipeline.[19]

Automated Tests: Write automated tests to ensure code quality and prevent regressions.[20]

Deployment Scripts: Create scripts to automate the deployment process to different environments.[21]

Infrastructure as Code: Use Infrastructure as Code (IaC) tools like Terraform or Ansible to manage and provision infrastructure.[22]

5. Best Practices

Start Simple: Begin with a basic CI/CD pipeline and gradually add more stages and complexity.

Automate Everything: Automate as many steps as possible to reduce manual effort and errors.[23]

Monitor and Improve: Continuously monitor your CI/CD pipeline and identify areas for improvement.[24]

Security: Integrate security checks into your pipeline to identify and address vulnerabilities.[25]

6. Example: CI/CD with GitHub Actions

YAML

```yaml
name: CI/CD


on:

  push:

    branches: [ main ]


jobs:

  build:

    runs-on: ubuntu-latest
```

```
steps:

  - uses: actions/checkout@v2

  - name: Install dependencies

    run:[26] composer install

  - name: Run tests

    run: vendor/bin/phpunit[27]

  - name: Deploy to server

    run: |

      # Add your deployment script here
```

This example demonstrates a basic CI/CD pipeline using GitHub Actions. It triggers on every push to the `main` branch, installs dependencies, runs tests, and then executes a deployment script.

By embracing CI/CD, you can accelerate your development process, improve code quality, and deliver software more efficiently.[28] Continuous feedback, automated testing, and streamlined deployments empower your team to focus on building great software and delivering value to users.[29]

www.ingramcontent.com/pod-product-compliance
Lightning Source LLC
LaVergne TN
LVHW051737050326
832903LV00023B/959